PORCELAIN BUTTERFLY

SCOTT RICHMAN

LIGHT SWITCH
PRESS

Published by:
Light Switch Press
PO Box 272847
Fort Collins, CO 80527

ISBN: 978-1-953284-07-5
Printed in the United States of America

BACK TO WRITING

Where am I, and where did I go?
My body went one way,
my soul did not follow.
I stand an empty vessel bare and hollow.

Withering away from the ground up.
Nothing has grown from this infertile soil;
no grass grows.

I can only acknowledge, because I do not understand.
How long I have walked this path only to discover
that I have not moved at all?

I think back only to observe that I am devoid of emotion.
Playing the game but going through the motion
of what life should be like.

But, I am here now to stand my ground.
To fertilize the very earth under my feet,
so that I and my surroundings survive.

10 HAIKU'S TO MAKE A POEM

Too sober to sleep
Not drunk enough to pass out
The room sits spinning

Dizzy spinning dreams
Reality make believe
I do not know which

Am I just crazy
The bottom of the bottle
My only friend now

I do not know how
But of course I justify
I know it's no use

So the same patterns
Lay on repeat and defeat
The person I am

I lay quivering
Thinking of past lives blaming
Of the price paying

From the till borrow
Precipice of my sorrow
Forgive and rejoice

Know when morning comes
Starting the day over now
We all have the choice

To be different
To sit with the repentance
With tears of lament

Know they can't torment
Any longer you're stronger
Now that you forgave

HAIKU #1

Powerful and grace
Fire dances around me
It touches my soul

A PANOPLY

Happily
    I'll adorn this panoply
Casually
    in a cage for your menagerie
Haphazardly
    tragically scorned warned not to be me
Nastily
    you cut me down like your child's plaything angrily
Sickening
    menacing footsteps quickening
Boastfully
    walk around like a butterfly socially
Narcissistically
    cataclysmically
Mournfully
    not regrettably set you free cathartically
Unapologetically
    name in lights on the marquis
Controversy
    you don't see what I see in my destiny
Illogically
    logical jubilee
Questioning
    it's my reckoning

Beckoning
        with a gale force summoning
Wondering
        why the fox is so cunning
Fanatically
        finically phonetically fumbling
Mumbling
        "What Does the Fox Say" humbly
Wandering
        around semi numbly
Sparingly
        sparkling spritely symphony
Panoply
        armor adorned tightly
Slightly
        scorned and burned frightfully
Faithfully
        for my friends and family
Shamefully
        never be ashamed it's honorably
Presently
        filled with glee for eternity
Gratefully
        thankfully sipping chamomile tea
Potpourri
        it's in a bowl right beside me
Sworn-fully
        on my honor it's my duty
Dutifully
        I'm on a killing spree

Joyfully
        spraying kind words ‘round “thank you” and “please”
Pleasingly
        like the ocean sea breeze
Baltic Sea
        every time I squeeze out a sneeze
Forensically
        chemically mind altering subconsciously
Probably
        along with the meta-physically
Lucidity
        or am I really even dreaming
Alchemy
        it’s my favorite anomaly
Metaphorically
        not when it comes to my truth and story
Maniacally
        manifesting my reality
Energetically
        I am technically speaking
Thinking
        but who am I for the teaching
Spiritually
        I am on a quest for the seeking
Beautifully
        live life to the fullest on the daily
Magically
        I thank everyone of you, you’re a blessing

PEACEFUL WINTER

When it snows, it's so peaceful and quiet.
Like the whitest, fluffiest cotton blanket
has just been pulled out of the closet
draped ever so gently over the earth;

with the squirrels and the birds
scurrying on the branches
while snow falls to the ground.

Do squirrels get cold in the winter,
and what do they do about splinters?

What about the trees?
It seems like they get so lonely;
they just seem more friendly with leaves.

The wind is calming like a whisper.
Just out of reach begging to be heard.
A tune never heard before,
but as old as time itself.

Coyotes sing in the distance
with melancholy reverence.
Deer graze where they play
and they lay after a hard day.

While children asleep in warm beds,
Sugar plum dreams dance in their heads.
Stuffed animals with swords
guarding their treasures.

It's so peaceful in winter,
but the snow glistens with forlorn teardrops.
Streets lay crying with the melting of the snow.
Their lamppost glow with a nod and a bow
of their heads in silence

WAKING FOREST

Walking into a forest I cleanse
My body with nature
Trees as tall as buildings guiding me
Ushering me ever deeper

As I walk my spirit gets lighter
With every breeze my body mind gain ease
Leaves falling circling
Transcending ever more presently
Mind altering ever so swiftly

Time moves forward as I move back
Out of the forest
I will have to keep this transcendental journey
With me
Coming out has changed me

I hope I do not forget

THE RENAISSANCE MAN

Long hair, long beard, sun worn, wrinkled skin.
Pipe smoke trickling out of his weathered pipe.
Writing away in a journal on a front porch
of the things he longs to share.

The sun shines bright on the man.
A light breeze across his skin.
That's how I wish it could be.
From everything I've ever seen.
But, alas, it could never be.
Never again be seen.

It's not what you are thinking.
This man on the porch,
not the one from long ago,
of the guy called Michael Angelo.
This man seemed from an age long passed,
I just saw him yesterday as I walked past.

It's my scene of the new renaissance man.

Where people await his newest book (or candy)
like little children await the praise of their parents.
In a life long passed he created a culture
that people hang on his every word;
his every dream that he could not make a reality.
Except for in a book, as he took a look,
where he could play out his own fantasy.

In a world full of technology
looking at the great writers of the past
could never be played out now.
What I mean, is being ruled by this thing
in our pocket is a whole world of possibility.
We are too consumed by what we see.
What we see is not reality, just make believe.
It takes away any of our future stability.

I wish this all could be played out again.
But, it cannot be unfortunately.
We have been programmed to consume.
If it doesn't grab our attention,
we make the small move
onto something new.
Too quickly we forget
nothing is ever new.

I long to have that life,
bold lines of strife
across my face.
Living life at such a slower pace.
Every word, every breath intentional.
Every day lived to be full.

The renaissance man knew who He was.

SLEEP

You lay awake in bed
Trying to get to sleep
Your mind keeps running
Thinking of something
But it's only one thing

....seconds....

....minutes....

....hours....

It goes through you all night
Finally sleeping never leaving
Morning comes too soon
Along with the thinking

The day brings change
Different thinking
Letting your mind
Take that break that it deserves
So you're not going crazy

Getting lost in the day
Mind wandering
Being dragged away
To another place
Finally not thinking

But then you get sleepy
Ready for bed
Coming back to reality
Oh! the sweet relief
Of all encompassing sleep!

Crawling into bed as you're not ready
Knowing what you've just been through
Feeling the deja vu
For it to come it's a tsunami
Tidal wave of thoughts come crashing in

And it begins all over again!

BAGGAGE

We all live
Things come
They go

Things come even though
You didn't want them to

Come and stay
Longer than planned

Sitting in the corner un-assumed
Though the weight a heavy burden
The unmasked box sitting forlorn

Mind plays tricks
Needing it there

We all have baggage
That needs unpacking
It needs sorting

Unlock the box
Peek inside
It won't bite

Remember the good
Forget the rest
They lay in the past

Realize they don't belong
Unburden the soul

Close the lid
It's all trash
Moving forward

Though, sometimes, it's still hard.

BURY THE HATCHET

Surrender the sirens
Surrender the flag
Bury the hatchet
Bury the flame

Forgive the past but never forget
Forward the happiness to the future
For you to see but never bet

Work at your own pace
Resolve your feelings
Finally seeing
Forgive the dwellings

Never give up
Never surrender

Resolution is happening
One day at a time
Resolving the problem
Lead us to peace

STUFFED ANIMALS

I have to sleep with my daughter's
Stuffed animal tonight
We call it "Kitty"
As I'm so lonely
Without you here
It's hard to bear
The emptiness in my chest
We've done this for almost a year

Somehow some nights seem like the first
Sleeping with no one else in the home
Some nights easy as others burst
Some nights filled full fright

No giggles or wiggles
No smiles while being put on trial
Meaningless shit to get me through another stent
Filling the void and hell bent
To see her again

Does this feeling fade?
Will it ever go away?

BY GRACE

knocked
pushed
thrown
I got pulled down
dragged
beat
broke

Dirt sand rocks kicked in my face
I got helped up humbled by the hands of grace
I brushed off the dirt brushed off the blame
I returned it by throwing love in their face

BLANK PAGES

Let's do something different
Rearranging the time we spent
On meaningless things
Of which nothing brings
Me out of the dark

Constant struggle
Spinning in the dark
With a straight jacket on
Always going nowhere fast

Like sitting in a row boat with one oar
Rowing as fast as I can
Spinning in circles
So I cannot plan
On where I'm going or where I end up

I wasn't supposed to talk about my bad days
Without me knowing I stopped talking
Because everyday was bad
For weeks on end crying was my new normalcy
It had been complacency replacing my only reality

I made it back from destruction
I'm alway under construction
From pad and pen
It got me out of the mindset
I strangely never knew I was in

So please I beg you do something
If you're not happy remember this one thing
You can always get out of the mess you're in

ROLLER COASTER

I've forgotten who I used to be and that's okay
for me. Because, at the end of the day,
I know life is a roller coaster of ups and downs.
At the end of each passing dawn,
there will be a chance to get to the top of the roller coaster.
I've learned that sometimes the falling is the best part of it.
Not knowing where you are going, but you're still alive.
You think the top is where you want to be.
The excitement, joy, fame, likes, follows it's all the same.
There's a price to pay. The falling is the best part.
The fall from expectations, the caring what other people think,
when you fall you are free.
Sometimes, that means you'll be
at the bottom for a while.
Just know that you'll be back
at the top one day.

Only this time you'll be who you need to be.

SCREW DRIVER

I'm turning the screw
Against the grain of wood
Slowly turning off my brain
Turning on my heart
Painful process but always a start
Turning the screw against society
One quarter turn at a time

WATER RIPPLES

Shadows of waters
Shallow and calm
Mist rolls over in the morning sun
I look into the water
I see the man I have become
Ripples in time show

Show the wrinkles on his face
I stare into the eyes
As I fall from grace
This is the man
Eyes shining bright as the universe
That will show me the way

CONQUERING TIDES

We have to take this one day at a time
We will always get through this together
Don't put this failure on me like it's mine
But I will always be right beside you

You think that I don't care
But I stay up late at night
Just wanting to know if you're alright

What you go through I will never know
Everybody's running from something

The tides come in like a tidal wave
Crashing down everything in path
They take the easiest path through
Taking the easiest way out

We are not the same we make change
We have the strength to pull through this
If we look to our friends around us
We get through any conquering tides

We run in circles biting our tail
End up doing nothing
Because we're too afraid to fail
What else is there to believe
All we have left now is family

Family over everything

SHADOW SELF

She walks in beauty
Only because she met herself
In the darkness the starkness
Learning to grow comfortable with loneliness

Walking beside her shadow
Her only friend on the mend
Prepared to go and grow
Around every bend

That is why she walks in beauty

DREAMING

I need to find my place in the world
I go from place to place always end up getting bored
I wish it could be so easy
I spend my days away in outer space dreaming
Of leaving to another time and place
I know if I got there everything would end up following me

But I still can't help the dreaming

SHOW ME THE WAY

I can't see the light
I can't see the light
Show me the way
I can't see the light
I can't see the light
It only comes from within you
Let it shine from your soul

CLOSED EYES

If I could close my eyes tight enough
Could this all be over

Throw the blankets and cover
Let the black blank void drown myself

And when I take the blankets off
Be in a different place

A different time
A different space

REAWAKEN

Reawaken my passion
Reawaken my soul
To fill the void the hole
In my head no future is dead
Dreams changing ever rearranging
Themselves to the new you
Sometimes it seems right to have no clue
All I knew what will always be true
Is that I am happy

TAKE BACK YOUR LIGHT

My demons have spoken and know my soul is broken

So back are my demons
Breathing down my back
Back for the attack
Stacked ready to crack
Open the door
Laid open the floor
From the bottom up it tore

Stacked with a vengeance
Vindictive torments descend
Down upon my guardian angels
They can only pretend
For so long before they get mangled
Tangled up in guerrilla warfare
Knuckles bleed crimson blood bare

Angels versus demons deceive us
Believe me I've seen this
Light versus dark
Sparks ignite
The dead of night quiet
An imbalance surrounds us
We cannot see yet not impervious

Negative energy flows and corrodes
As the energy field surrounding bows
Awaiting to implode
From shear density
Vast immensity

I take back my light
This is not the time to be polite
I take back my love
Guardian angels surround from above
This is the time to be tough
Though the path doesn't have to be rough

STARS OF TWILIGHT

The stars at twilight
Still aren't that bright
Overshadowed by the sunlight
Doesn't take from their spotlight
At night

The Stars have their time
To shine in their prime
Of chasmic sublime
A new paradigm
I climb

In the evanescence
Of their distance
And renaissance
Not by chance
They dance

And the bunnies play in the grass

EAGLES

Words have such a mystical power
They make you curl up in a tight ball
Or they let you tower over all
Make you dead in the head
Regretting everything you have ever said
They make you feel alive
When everything is against you
Making you shout out your very truth
Because it needs to be heard
Or you keep it all inside
Following everybody else in the same herd
Flocking together as birds
Be the eagle flying alone
It just does it's never shown
The tide raises all boats
Let the words be the tide
The power of the ocean
Raise all those around him
Words have such a wonderful power
You get to make somebody or break somebody

You decide

HOUSE ON THE MOON

If I could have a house on the moon
just to get away from it all,
it could never be too soon
the space is never too tall.

Just for a moment in time
would the world see that I'm gone?
Where did this life go that was mine?
I sensed it was all a con.

I sit on the moon as it's so lonely up here.
I saw a woman with kids in a backyard and fence.
A window opened up, so I could see more clear.
Is this the present or future? It didn't make sense.

It was sometime in the fall, but the scene started to disappear.
Me and this woman were sitting with a blanket too small.
We had grown older together with gray in our hair;
we had lines in our face but still happy and all.

Now, I want to get down to get off of this thing!
What is this hell that I'm in, what is this hell I abhor?
I want that movie, or future, to stop haunting me.
Turn on the lights, stop the projector, this isn't happy anymore.

As I look back on what I could have had
will I ever get that life or did I realize too late?
Hindsight is always twenty-twenty, now let me just be a dad.
Was it the right choice or was it all fate?

I guess I screwed up but how will I ever know?
To have a house on the moon isn't impressive at all.
To have a wife and kids that's the ultimate show,
what else do I have before the final bugle call?

Now, I don't want a house on the moon.
I want to be there with you.
Getting off of this thing, will never be too soon.
I guess the time had past before I had knew.

THE PHOENIX

It's a new dawn it's a new day
I can be anything I want to be
I can now be anything that my heart can see
Take the best and push away the rest
Leaving the bad behind me
Be grateful that I am blessed
I am watching the old me burning
To the ground from the ashes

I am a phoenix

Each burning is a turning of the tides
Shedding away all the lies
From the ashes I rise
A better version of me

BLESSINGS

I wish that I could write like I used to.
The littlest, shortest stories that came out like they were supposed to.
I grabbed on to the idea loosely, letting it flow through.
I held on white knuckled not prepared, but excited,
        where it would end.
Always, mystifying myself and thankful for the blessing.
I may not write like I used to.
Though, everything still comes out like it's supposed to.

As always,
        Thankful for the Blessing

GOD

God is within us all
not an external source
the more you look inside
and know yourself
the more you know
and are closer to god

HAIKU #5

Like dust in shadows
As well as deer in meadows
I am never seen

LOOKING BACK ON NATIVE AMERICAN LAND

The leaves and sticks rushed under my feet
Wind blowing behind my back
As she sang they came to join in
Kids playing in the fields at first
I look around and see the ancestors of this land
Came to join hands and band together as one

SILENCE

I sit here in silence.
Thinking of the world's violence;
the violence inside me.
What can we do to control it?
Love and compassion is what we,
as a human race need.
Love more, do more, just for you.
To do it for anyone else
you've been played the fool.
You only hurt yourself, your soul.
It is said you live the next life of the person you've hurt.
In the moment of weakness abort
the violence and replace it with love.
Makes you a better person and rising above
the hatred in the world and all the cruel evil injustice.
Live for you, though, not by the fool.
Not by the weakness, no ignorance is not bliss.
Ignorance is just a thought, a kiss,
by death.

THE MIND'S GARDEN

He's trapped inside his own imprisoned mind.
Padded walls, metal door, and straight jacket bind.
Sleeping alone on the cold floor.
His thoughts are his only friend he gets to explore.

Pride and ego kept him alive.
Now, they won't let him thrive.
Holding him back against his will.
Dined and dashed leaving him with the bill.

He's paid the price that lead him here.
Left him in ruins, face full of tear.
Struggle, remorse, burdened with fear.
Lessons learned and some bridges burned clear.

Not burned; exploded with the magnitude
of a thousand sticks of dynamite imbued
in a controlled demolition of his mind's sight.
The very second he said "go" with smiled delight.

Now, alone on an island,
he gets to grow the beautiful flowers of grand
as he's only seen in paintings on tall
museum walls and castle halls.

Planting a garden in his mind,
he will not be defined.
His mind held the key
that will set him free.

STARLIGHT

Let's lay here under the starlight
From the fading skylight
Fingers trace all God's grace
Hold each other's embrace
Will you lay here on this blanket
Hand in hand as we enjoy it
For hours made of flannel
Looking at the endless panel
Of star maps that lay before us
Let's forget the fuss
Of the day
While we lay
Head on my chest
Always forever blessed
Talking away through the night
Everything and nothing that might fright
Though we may fight and bicker
While the flame may flicker
Forgetting past blames
Use our passion to fan the flames
Choose each other every single day
Over and over before we decay

Before we smolder into ash

THE PENSIEVE

I've found a new passion
Found a new flame
Although it will never
Give me the fame
I do not seek

I wish that I could write like the great poets of past
But most days when my pen hits paper
I have to fight to just sound like me
And then to me I just sound like an infant

But nevertheless I keep scratching away
With quill on paper
I have to get these thoughts out
To make room

Writing to me is like putting a wand to my temple
To extract the memory burned forever in my mind
But those memories bind me they blind everything
I only want to think about them on my own time
Not every waking moment of my fucking life

I force my quill to slides across
The paper unfolding my thoughts
That I might wish to still keep secret
For some reason I keep writing

I do not write for you
I might not even write for me
I do not know

The words just need to get out of my mind
So I might be able to think properly clearly
Or whatever it might be
But if only for a moment in time

So I will keep sliding quill across paper
Not knowing until later what's in my mind
I write to find out

SURRENDERING

Let go and surrender
To the good times remember
What has came and gone
Along the way but now alone
It happened for a reason
It was only for a season

In this life
Should be no strife
Along the path a stepping stone
Divine timing you will be shown
For reasons right now
You will not know

Everything happens for a reason

ERASE THE LINE

If I could just step over the line of fear
How far could I go
How high could I reach
It's just a line drawn in the sand

Erase it with your feet

SEASON: FALL

Turning yellow
Orange
Red
Falling to the ground
Trees shed their leaves
Pound for pound
They are not dead
Ever changing
Ever rearranging
Finally seeing the forest
Through the trees
Finally being able to see
Letting go is beauty
Making room to grow
To their next phase on the journey
No loss
No mourning
No tears
No fears
They let go of what's holding them back
They know when it's time to let go
Recognize the beauty

HAIKU #6

Love Pumping in veins
Fireworks light across night
Instantly with you

THE FIELDS

He saw her standing there in wonder from afar
In a field full of death nothing grows
Her hair flows from the wind
Sun graces her face

She looked intriguing in her sunglasses
How could she stand there in wonder
When there is nothing to look at
He could not imagine how

The surrounding lands were all so bland
Everything dead different shades of brown
Everything on the ground
Even the grass was lifeless

Nothing was taller than the girl
Except the occasional tree
That broke in half with the peak hanging upside down
Maybe not even touching the ground
This field had been like this far longer than a lifetime's lifetime

Yet with all of that she took in
She still stood there in wonder
In fascination rumination
He had to know the secret

As he moved closer he could not see
Until he was standing right beside her
She never knew he existed
He saw it coming from deep within
It showed in her eyes projecting on her sunglasses
The greenest fields he had ever seen
The lushest patches of fruit and berries
Multicolored flowers
Nothing dead was there
Nobody would have ever known
What that patch of land had been through

She could see the land for what it was
She was the only one willing to give love
To the ground when no one else would

How do I do this to myself again
To tear my walls down and let you in?

PORCELAIN BUTTERFLIES

Again, depression fits hits
like a ton of bricks.
From every small dip
will it ever quit?

And I'm slumped over, and hunched over,
hunch backed and side tracked
in need of a four leaf clover.

So, I don't crossover
to the other side of life.
I wish I had a rainbow and butterfly
to fly over to the sunshine.

I'm in the coal mine.
Where's the diamond in the rough?
I need to call my own bluff,
but it's tough hanging on by boot straps and handcuffs.

Chained to misery and I see

light at the edge of the tunnel.
Give me my pickaxe with cart on tracks.
Flood the place and build a channel;
float on through in the cracks.

A porcelain butterfly, beautiful, and bold.
In the wrong hand's breakable and too cold to hold.
I hold on still in need as I bleed beads of blood,
yet, I stood standing in a mountain of gold
without ever knowing.

Knowing and growing that now starts the flowing.
The flowing of the river cascading through my heart.
I just need the courage to start.
Nothing can tear my heart apart.

My life is broken. I'll fix it with kintsugi.
Golden glue mends, bends and sinks in
to celebrate the broken pieces that make me true.
I am now whole, again.

Now, behold my heart,
it can't be torn apart.
Now, I can restart

my life.

QUARANTINE

I might be down and out
Right now but not down for the count
I've still got to get through the next twelve rounds
Left in the ring
To dance and sing
To "float like a butterfly"
And to "sting like a bee"
Fight for the happiness to be free

I know we're all struggling
In this time of apocalyptical quarantine
But that's not stopping me
From being overly judging
On myself but this is probably just a test
That I'll have to fight for the rest
Of my life and I'll fight with the best

I've seen my worth
Since the day of my birth
Yet I can't seem to get things right
Still everyday I fight the good fight
No stopping no end in sight

I'll pick myself up with my chin held high
And I let the tears roll down my face when I cry
There's no reason to bury my face and hide
Because it's ok for men to show emotion
Being vulnerable is a magical potion

Don't bottle them up any longer
It will truly make me stronger
Accepting the pain takes away the anger
Taking away the stranger
Inside of me I didn't know
Yet to the world I let it show
Now I have to let him go

It might be hard
But I have to let down my guard
And show the world the true me

That I will be happy even if I'm struggling

NOT FINISHED YET

I'm shedding my demons
Shedding my skin
Shedding the things that have worn me thin

Breaking free of what's surrounding me
The shackles around my ankles weighing me down
Are now broken lay on the ground

I burn in the fires rising stronger from the ashes
Blood runs down my back from the forty lashes
Blessed by the angels being able to find every angle

Don't count me out of the bet
No I'm not finished just yet

SEARCHING...

I wake up everyday wishing I could do something different
Then I go ahead and slam my head upon the pavement
They say insanity is doing things
Over and over and over and over
Expecting different results

All I am doing is blowing that wish a kiss
Sending it on the wings of a prayer
In a hope that it comes back like a boomerang
And if it did it probably missed by miles

I don't know if I'll ever be able to find it
But I'll keep searching with blood sweat and tears
Hoping above all hope through all of my fears

That I keep searching

BLOOD FAMILY

Blood doesn't just mean family
Remember that when you think of me
You had claimed family over everything
Apparently it ends when we disagree

Here I am sorry to see you go
Maybe we can be friends again
Someday soon it will begin again
But I won't ever really know

My intent was just my heart was pure
Can you say the same
You have listened but didn't hear
Our communication just wasn't clear

You sit there preaching
But only thinking
About your lives
Wanting only one thing
But cannot see
What lies beneath
What we've been through
Played like the fool

You see your minds lies
You gave up with no try
Angry words with a fight
Leading ourselves to demise

You won't crawl back to me
But set aside the pride
Slowly start again our family
Bringing you back to reality
So we can have family over everything

BURNED BRIDGES

The bridges that burned
The friendships that turned
Have guided me through the night
Guiding me with the light

You controlled my life for way too long
To you I have never belonged
So now I have cut the ties
Severing all the lies from your eyes

It's hard to see you go my friend
But we'll both be stronger in the end
So now we can begin
To start our new life again

So I let you go to see the pain flow
Out of my body out of my life go
The pain that you put me through
I'm not afraid to let you go too

For the first time I have listened to my heart
I'm the only one that can tear it apart

It's not selfish
It's not selfish
I need to let you go

FEELIN' GOOD

I'm living life again
Like it's my high again
She's in my sky again
Flashing diamonds again

Teetering tots
Weathering plots
A storms a brewing
Don't wanna go back to losing

I need an umbrella to shield the rain
I need the warmth to quell the pain

But I feel it in my bone
When will it be gone
When will it be done
Go back to being fun

Tornado twisted twisting temple
Could it really be so simple
Formulation not rumination
Make a plan to cultivate the motivation

When did this begin again
Did I find my true self again
I'm living life again
Like it's my high again

High roller wearing shoes of a bowler
Casual stroller strolling strong controller
Soaking up all the solar
Rays on my face like I'm a steamroller
The clouds have parted
And I just started
To run my race
My own terms my own pace

Coming out of the other side strong
Skipping like I own this place
That I belong

AS MY DAUGHTER SLEEPS

Oh! be still my heart
The tears are about to start
I know you are sleeping
Looking ever so peacefully
The joy and happiness
That you exude to me
Take my ego away
Without ever knowing it
You have shown me the way through
Life sacrifices made all for you
It does not matter now
I am your father
You are my daughter
I just hope you know
How much I love you

CUT THE CHAIN

Round and round and round it goes
Where I stop nobody knows
When will I have to let go
Is this friend or really foe

For far too long I've held on tight
I've tried with all my might
For things to turn out just right
All endings came with fight

Struggles fear and pain
No longer friends to gain
I have to let go to retain
All my sanity that's left to remain sane

In your hands the cards you show
With the river your chance you blow
You always reap what you sow
You always have dragged me in tow

I'm glad you're out of my sight
And frankly it's quite alright
I'll take flight with this kite
Soar into the deepest depths of night

With the cutting of the chain
You are no longer the constrain
You can never contain
You can never again be the bane

Of my existence that I now reclaim

TIME

Ocean waves crash intricate
Patterns on the sand
Heart beats intoxicate
Lovers hand in hand
Melancholy's indoctrinate

Forlorn shadows
Whisper breath winds
Creep along meadows
Sun nigh cleanse
Teardrop gallows

Father Time's clock
Sweeping in time
Talks in tick tock
Gives signs rewind
Broken time walk

Fire furnace flurries
Sinking of the moon
Sun beams buries
Desert sand dune
Quasar quest queries

Mother Earth's flower
All connections one
Energetic power
Knowing we won
On castle tower

Time stands still for no man

HAIKU #7

No trees on the plains
Happy arborist plants seeds
Johnny Appleseed

ODE TO SOCKS

There's nothing like a brand new pair of socks
So fluffy and fuzzy wrapped in a smile
Once open the old ones lay
In the back of the drawer forgot

Although you don't remember
Because you've just opened
A love letter to you feet

They aren't worn and thin
No holes no threads being exposed
So you can feel the shoe through
Or the cold from the floor

That's the whole point of socks
That they block your feet from everything

I opened a love letter to my feet this morning

NOSTALGIA

The full moons face shines down
The push and pull of the ocean water
The budding of the flowers and trees
Crisp cool air on the nose

Fire smoke bellows from chimney
Old memories come to surface
Perfumes of the past outlast
The present moment

The campfire sings songs of symphony
Crackle pop of nostalgia
Toasted marshmallows burnt
Laid on gram cracker bed

Tells stories of tales
Leaving trails in our head
Nature calls all around us
Can we be called back

To a childish state of wonder
Waving to our friend
The imaginary is real
And the moon smiles back down upon us

LIVE YOUR LIFE

Your life's just begun
It's far from being over
Take it day to day
Pretty soon you'll be older

Never get those chances back
Dreaming of nights so black
Looking in the mirror
Look inside have faith
It's only you too blame

Times are changing of the American way
I'm only dreaming of seeing the day
When they are different and never a slave
To their work getting little pay

Never reaping the rewards
Never getting their benefits
Just making the rich richer
And letting the poor drown

So be the change you want to see
Change the world how you want it to be
Don't do it just to please the people you meet
Do it for yourself and you will see
That's all it takes to be free

So live for today
Live for today
And you won't have to pray
For love to come another way

Live for today
Live for today
You won't have to pray
To live the spirits way

NEVER SAY NEVER

I should have known to never say never.
Not now, or ever until forever.
Stop using that word for worse or better.
Now, that's how to be sufficiently clever.

You may not want but, things can change in an instant.
One thing's for sure, there is no constant.
Constrain, struggle, maintain humble.
Words are poison tend to fumble, tumble, and crumble.
Finicky, frailties of future reality.
Causing strain, extreme anxiety.

There's got to be more to life than this.
More than the everlasting bliss,
Of the normal high society.
Living in the throws of almighty piety.

There may come a day
In more than one way.
You have to go back on your word.
Your vision got too screwed up and blurred.

Just know that it's for the best,
The magic on your life it has blessed.

When I Was Younger

When I was eight, I had the whole world in front of me.
I could be anything that my eyes could see.
Whatever it was, that I could put my hands on,
no matter what or where I had come from.

I could only reach so high with imagination so wild,
with all my future ahead of me it took me like fire.

So, now, I sit here settling in my path.
Have I forgotten what it meant
to have the flame deep from within?

Is it still the same as when I was younger
and do I still have the world ahead of me?
Am I lost and can I find myself,
will I ever find my way again?

I wish it could be the same as back then.
So care free with the world ahead of me.
I know I'm still young but what do I know?
How fast we grow and little we know.

Will I be the same now as fifty?
Thinking I wish I could be twenty.
I could know more and am willing to learn.
Will it be too late with nowhere to go?

That seems so long in the future.
How fast will that time go?
Do I have the time to plan out where I end?
Will I wake up and just wonder how that time was spent?

INTERNAL DEBATE

You sit there on a chair in a depressed state.
A struggle inside you, internal debate.
Two sides come crashing, come clashing
From what has been done.
You've blocked out the sun
from inside you, no internal energy.
Pick up a pen, write down what you are thinking,
in that moment of blinking
comes clarity, no more pity,
no more fidgeting.

Feel the sun, moon, earth, and wind.
The balance of energy, an almighty blend.
Use it as one restoring the chi.
The push the pull of the ocean by moon,
the eternal flame by the sun.
Grounded by rocks to not move in your choices
from the negativity created by the voices.
Let the wind clear those thoughts.
Be at peace in this time and place.
Be at peace so you can come to face,
The real you, the you at peace.

MEMORIES

I remember. I remember that day.
I remember that day like it was yesterday.
That infamous day you shoved me away.
The many shows we should have played.
The memories that were never made.

But it seems, but it seems you're ok.
You're ok with the choices you made.
How quick you are to judge none of the facts.
How quick you are to turn your back.

The devils in the details which you don't have.
Casting judgement among me seemingly glad.
Too selfish to realize you're burning bridges.
Apparently, made dead those long friendships.

You won't realize until it's too late.
With you in a house all alone.
Wondering why no one is around.
When you're the only one in the home.

Thinking to yourself what went wrong?
Deep down you knew all along,
That you weren't happy only jealous;
Taking the frustration out on us.

Let it be, let it be.
Let it be and be at peace.
You are angry, angry at me.
What about all those memories
We made together as a family?

Let it go, let it go.
Let it go no one cares anymore.
Just you and your selfish soul.
Let it go, let it be.
Let it go and be at peace.

MMMHMMM

I know that history repeats
When empires fall to the ground
What if we can change the world
With the music we have found

We all change we all grow
From the hope of a seed
To the people we meet
And things we believe

Our past doesn't control the future
It's the things that we do
We control the future
Let our actions speak loud!

Just sit by idle with the world passing by
Doing nothing kills you quicker
But that only makes me sicker
Go home and slit your wrist
Get it over with faster

Write that song
Paint the picture
Take your camera
Everywhere you go
What you do now
Has an effect
On everyone else

Now go out and change your work
You know what this is about
You've heard what I've said
Change the world

I AM THE SAND

I am the sand
I am the time in the hour glass
That falls through your hand
I too shall pass

Fleeting essence
Dire consequence
No romance
Action figure screwed in stance

Askew on shelf
No foot loose
A loss of self
When did I choose

This path this life this place
I hear the angels talks
Amongst themselves in time and space
An echo of the ticks and the tocks of the clocks

Sweeping seemingly too swift
I am afraid of the pain I gain won't stain
Enough for me to shift
Gears and my life cannot change

Will I refuse to be used
Caged inside a refuge
Water sweeping deluge
I will not be used

House made of cards
Broken mirror glass shards
With no disregards
Crystal wards safeguards

AM I WEAK

Am I weak?
The things that I speak
Are different than the things that I think
Am I about to break?

Am I awake?

Mind wants spring
It's wants spring to be sprung
Where it doesn't belong
Am I even listening?

Body wants thunderstorms of rain
That flower the gardens of seeds
Of weeds that cause more pain
In the end

How will I ever know
If that garden isn't tilled so
Properly picked pansies can propagate
The flower bed

Am I weak?

MY DARK PASSENGER

The darkness that may have come to light
The darkness that may have come to fight
This is the time this is the place
This is the time you have to face
The demon within us all— that one dark passenger
This is our final fight or our final flight
To get to the light to get out of the blight
You must know the past to conquer the future
This is the time to leave it all behind

HAIKU #9

Stars looks bright tonight
And as I look at the sight
I feel whole again

FREEDOM OF EXPRESSION

Co-wrote by Leon Jones

Freedom of expression is a progression
That's the objection for confession
You have to do you in every obsession
That's the ultimate lesson in decompression

That can lead to aggressive rejection hard for digestion

Because no matter what someone will disagree
They will throw shades of incarnate rage across every page
No matter what you will come to see
That you cannot please everyone eventually

Paying for slaying saying your opinions aren't facts
So you lay tiptoeing tactics for troubling tacts
No matter what side your on forty lashes to your back
From the other side of the tracks wolves gather in packs

There will be more sessions of possession
With the repression of suppression
There is a confession that has to be made for progression
Or that leads to a greater rapacious oppression

So we march on, strong arm,
Verbally stepping to make impression,
Words are weapons to those in opposition to progression,
Constantly stressing to keep free speech in suppression!

We ring freedom of expression!

A fire inside is steady raging, full engagement
As artists you can't hold creatives to enslavement!
You wont hold us down! This is history in the making!
We all breathe and bleed free, so why put a lock on being opinionated?
What's worse?! Being melanated feeling enslaved, and indoctrinated!

The chains must be broken and forsaken!

See I'm all for unity! Pure community! Diversity!
So why try to divert the peace?
Oh Lord mercy me! Try and see,
Differences, just expand a more colorful tapestry.
Make lavishly what it means to be free! think without legality!
When our very thoughts have capacity to shape new realms of reality!

@livingcanvas84_ Leon Jones

Leon Jones loves art in all its forms, and skillfully employs it to challenge, evoke thought, support and motivate. Art is in his blood, and his being exudes and expresses it. If he's not expressing himself through writing poetry, songs, and inspirational messages, he is doing so by singing and dancing like nobody's watching, A Motivational speaker and supporter for Disability Advocacy, In 2010, he was awarded Advocate of the Year and The Spirit of Detroit Award. Born in New Jersey, he now resides in Michigan.

ANXIETY INDUCED VERTIGO

Rumbling tumbling
Forever mumbling
Forever numb
My brain
No ears can hear
No noise can queer broken thoughts
Twisted knots padlocks
Transfixed spots
Wave crash rocks
Trapped inside memory box
Dizzy spinning daydreams
Reality make believe
Never see
Floating sea
No void commotion
Endless ocean
Forever distance
Standing still
Never moving this spot
Little dot
Blurb on radar
Been too far
Door never shut ajar
No pills thrills frills
Only spills
Body + floor = one
Ache-less aches
Oxygen brain masquerade
Power-aide can't power through
What to do
Sleep drink bottles up

Smoke it up
Toke it up
Maybe just a little bump
For a little bit

Soon you'll have to quit
Take a moment to actually process it
Grieving is the first step to fleeting
Colossus releasing Cathartically
Leading to the believing

The only thing is to know you're a human being
Maybe your heart's content but still bleeding
Not the only one going through this thing
Now just slowly start breathing
Inhale ://: exhale
Eyes closed and thinking
Now you should only be saying to yourself this one thing

"I am grateful to be alive"

YOUR GAZE

Percolations of insinuations from your eyes
lead me to believe all the lines
that you spouted from tongue, teeth, and lip.
From your crazy hips.
That certain way they dip.

The essence of the scent
from your skin
submits me to wounded knee bent.
Powerful prayer of mercy
Can't even begin
to describe my plea's sent

Oh! But your gaze!

Your gaze is dangerous, insidious,
meticulous, wildly conspicuous
ever so luscious.

I digress,
it takes away from the story of my goddess.

A galaxy of heaven; a nebula,
a supernova of love.
Sent from heavens above.

Your gaze, a blaze,
a fiery inferno.
That sets the paint into glaze
and incinerates my doubts fears and ego.
Sends me into a daze for days.

Your eyes lead me into actually believing
that I am a good human being and leading
a life that I deserve and that's a blessing.

Your gaze is wicked and I am blessed.

Made in the USA
Coppell, TX
30 August 2020

34758638R00046